W9-CAW-848

Table of Contents

Photographs in this book show the life cycle of a monarch butterfly.

egg

4

The Life Cycle of a

Butterfly

by Lisa Trumbauer

Consulting Editor: Gail Saunders-Smith, Ph.D.

Consultant: Ronald L. Rutowski, Professor, Department of Biology, Arizona State University

Pebble Books

an imprint of Capstone Press
North Mankato, Minnesota

Pebble Books are published by Capstone Press
1710 Roe Crest Drive, North Mankato, Minnesota 56003
www.capstonepub.com

Library of Congress Cataloging-in-Publication Data

Trumbauer, Lisa, 1963—
    The life cycle of a butterfly / by Lisa Trumbauer.
    p. cm.—(Life cycles)
    Includes bibliographical references (p. 23) and index.
    Summary: Simple text and photographs present the life cycle of a butterfly.
    ISBN-13: 978-0-7368-1181-1 (hardcover)
    ISBN-10: 0-7368-1181-8 (hardcover)
    ISBN-13: 978-0-7368-3390-5 (softcover pbk.)
    ISBN-10: 0-7368-3390-0 (softcover pbk.)
    1. Butterflies—Life cycles—Juvenile Literature. [1. Butterflies—Life cycles. 2.
Caterpillars.] I. Title. II. Life cycles (Mankato, Minn.)
QL544.2.T78 2002
595.78′9—dc21   2001004840

Note to Parents and Teachers

The Life Cycles series supports national science standards related to
life science. This book describes and illustrates the life cycle of a
[monarch] butterfly. The photographs support early readers in
understanding the text. The repetition of words and phrases helps
early readers learn new words. This book also introduces early
readers to subject-specific vocabulary words, which are defined in
the Words to Know section. Early readers may need assistance to
read some words and to use the Table of Contents, Words to
Know, Read More, Internet Sites, and Index/Word List sections
of the book.

Printed in the United States of America in Eau Claire, Wisconsin.
061715   009048R

A butterfly begins life
as an egg.

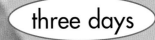
three days

A caterpillar hatches from the egg. The caterpillar eats the egg shell.

caterpillar

8

The caterpillar eats
many leaves. The
caterpillar grows quickly.

The caterpillar molts.
It sheds its outer skin
to grow.

chrysalis

The caterpillar hangs upside down. It molts into a chrysalis.

butterfly

A butterfly comes out of
the shell of the chrysalis
after about two weeks.
Butterflies can live
for nine months.

A male butterfly courts
a female butterfly.
The two butterflies mate.

18

The female butterfly lays many eggs. She puts one on each leaf.

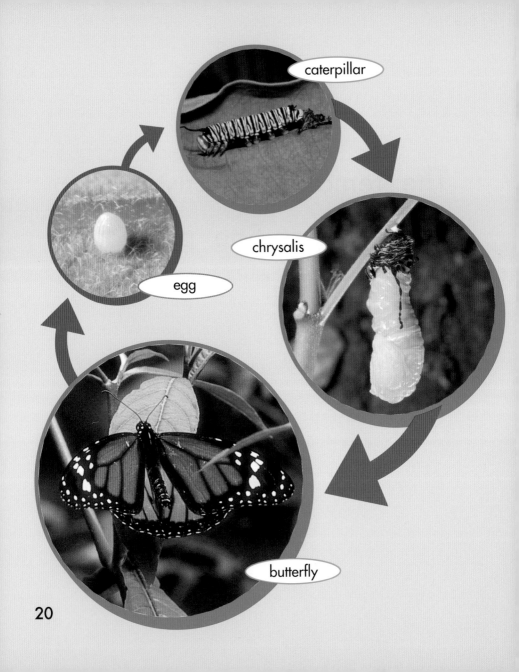

caterpillar

egg

chrysalis

butterfly

The egg is the start
of a new life cycle.

(Words to Know

caterpillar—a worm-like larva that hatches from an egg and molts often; caterpillar is the second life stage of a butterfly.

chrysalis—a pupa covered by a hard shell; chrysalis is the third life stage of a butterfly.

court—to attract for mating

egg—a small case in which a caterpillar grows; egg is the first life stage of a butterfly.

hatch—to break out of an egg shell

life cycle—the stages of being born, growing up, having young, and dying

mate—to join together to produce young

molt—to shed skin so that new skin can grow; caterpillars molt several times as they grow and change form.

shell—a hard covering around an egg; caterpillars eat the shells of their eggs.

22

Read More

Bauman, Amy, and E. Jaediker Nosgaard. *The Wonder of Butterflies.* Animal Wonders. Milwaukee: Gareth Stevens, 2000.

Frost, Helen. *Caterpillars.* Butterflies. Mankato, Minn.: Pebble Books, 1999.

Lerner, Carol. *Butterflies in the Garden.* New York: HarperCollins, 2001.

Internet Sites

FactHound offers a safe, fun way to find Internet sites related to this book.

Go to *www.facthound.com*

Fact Hound will fetch the best sites for you!

Index/Word List

Word Count: 101
Early-Intervention Level: 13

Editorial Credits

Martha E. H. Rustad, editor; Jennifer Schonborn, production designer and interior illustrator; Kia Bielke, cover designer; Kimberly Danger, Mary Englar, and Jo Miller, photo researchers

Photo Credits

Ann and Rob Simpson, 18
Barrett and MacKay, 16, 20 (bottom)
Dwight R. Kuhn, 10, 20 (top)
Robert & Linda Mitchell, cover (inset)
Unicorn Stock Photos/Ron Holt, cover, 6, 14
Visuals Unlimited/David Cavagnaro, 1; Dick Poe, 4, 20 (left); Bill Beatty, 8; William J. Weber, 12, 20 (right)